First published 1992 in Great Britain by
EAJ PUBLICATIONS
18 Chapel Street, Astwood Bank,
Redditch, Worcestershire, B96 6DA.

Copyright © 1992 Ann Jones

ISBN 0 951921 0 0 2

No part of this book may be reproduced in any form
without the publisher's prior consent in writing.

Cover and book design by Clive Moss.

'Seek and Ye Shall Find'

'When the Pupil is Ready the Teacher Appears'

ANN JONES

A WAY OF LIFE

EAJ Publications

Contents

Acknowledgments 5

Introduction 6

1 How it all began... 7

2 Spirit communication 12

3 Working as a medium 15

4 Is there life after death? 18

5 Karma and reincarnation 20

6 Colours of the aura 23

7 Psychic and spiritual experiences 25

8 The Zodiac and the new age 30

9 The Tarot 32

10 Gemstones and crystals 35

11 Conclusion 38

Recommended reading 39

Useful addresses 40

Glossary 41

I would like to thank my husband Eddie for his support and patience, Elsie for opening up my pathway to spiritual development, and Dorothy and Malcolm without whose help this book would not have been published in this form.

Introduction

I have written this book in response to many requests from people who have attended my talks or who have come to me for consultations. I want to share with them my thoughts and experiences in order that they may be helped to develop their own spirituality.

However, no one person can provide all the answers, least of all me, but I can share my development in the hope that it will encourage others to open their minds to external influences which exist outside the physical body, and therefore stimulate their search for spiritual awakening.

It is my experience that once a person is drawn to the psychic field, the search for knowledge becomes an endless quest; it is like opening Pandora's box. There are scores of pathways to tread, for example *Spiritualism, Christian Science and Theosophy.* There is no doubt that we all have a spark of curiosity within us and when it starts to come alight it will set us on the quest to find ourselves and the God within.

My experience has shown that organised religion can close the mind to spiritual development by not encouraging questioning and reasoning. We must realize that whichever pathway we take, whichever association, cult or church we embrace, there is only one God, but there are many pathways to the Godhead. If all religions awoke to this truth then the brotherhood of man would truly be here.

Finally I have endeavoured in this book to relate explanations of various psychic terms to personal experience, and where possible to explain what is happening around us at the dawn of this *New Age.*

1 How it all Began

Even as a small child I was psychic, although I didn't realize it at the time. I was an only child, never spoilt, in fact I was brought up quite strictly. At first we lived with my grandmother so that my parents could look after her. I slept in an attic bedroom in which there was an old trunk full of sheets and blankets. When I was lying in bed at night the trunk sometimes opened, and what I can only describe as 'things' would emerge.

I know now that I was experiencing psychic phenomena, but as a child I was scared, and would go and awaken my parents. Their reaction was typical; I was told not to be silly and to go back to sleep. Eventually however my parents gave in and moved me into their bedroom, but the psychic activity did not end there. Sometimes I felt that I had become very large, and at other times I thought that I was sitting on the top of the wardrobe looking down at my own body; I saw people that nobody else could see. I now understand that these were out-of-the-body experiences, and the people I saw were spirit people.

I was born during the war years on December 22nd 1942, the night of a full moon. I always felt different as a child and did not make friends easily. I was frequently ill, very nervous and very sensitive, but I loved animals and felt more in tune with them than with people. I was also very much a book worm and adored reading.

The years passed and when I was about ten years old my grandmother died. My parents moved into a flat, which I thought was wonderful; it had all mod cons. No more baths by the coal fire once a week, and no more looking in the outside toilet for spiders. For a short time my psychic experiences disappeared, then they began again.

I was very fond of our boxer dog *Tina*. I always came home from school at lunchtime to take her out for a walk. Although I was a 'latch key' child, I never had to come home to an empty house because Tina was always there to greet me. When Tina died I was heartbroken.

The day after Tina died, I came home from school to see her sitting on the mat chewing her bone. She wagged her tail, as she always did when she saw me.
I stroked her, cuddled her and cried with joy because she had not left me. Of course I told my parents, but they were not able to see her and thought I was being silly again. That night I felt Tina get onto my bed, and over the following weeks I saw her many times. Gradually I began to cease grieving over her. By the time I was in my teens we had bought another dog and had moved to the Greenlands estate in another part of Redditch.

I enjoyed my teenage years. I had a close friend called *Betty* and we enjoyed each others company. However during that time I experienced many strange happenings which I could not understand. I had to walk about half a mile to Betty's house, and during that time I always felt that I had someone with me. I could hear footsteps walking with me, the faster I walked the quicker the footsteps walked. I could not wait to get home and shut the front door behind me. I also experienced dancing lights around me, especially when the footsteps were around. Although as a teenager this frightened me, I now realize that I had spirit protection.

It was about this time that my bedroom was redecorated, and I was allowed to choose the wallpaper. I chose a pattern of white feathers on a blue background. My parents thought that I had gone mad, but that was the wallpaper I wanted, and I was insistent. I will be explaining the significance of the choice later in the book.

At the age of eighteen I was involved in an accident which was to change my whole life. I was due to go to France with the local youth club, but the previous night I went out with some friends and was involved in a terrible car accident. My nose and jaw were broken, my skull fractured, and I received over a 100 stitches to my face. I should have been at the *Hotel Eden* in France, instead I was in *Eden Ward, Stratford-on-Avon Hospital !*

I was badly scarred. I could not go out and spent much of the next twelve months in and out of hospital. I lost a year of my life. Due to the remarkable skills of a surgeon at the Queen Elizabeth Hospital Birmingham, my face was repaired by skin grafting and plastic surgery, and I was able to start living again.

Eighteen months later I married *Eddie*. I now have two daughters who share the same birthday, June 15th, *Kirsty* having arrived four years after *Karen*.

From the time of the accident my psychic experiences had ceased, however I had this one manifestation on the day that Kirsty was born. I woke up at five o' clock in the morning, feeling just as I had as a child, huge and floating above my body, looking down on myself. I felt sure that the baby would be born that day and so I woke up my husband. I had no labour pains and no indications of imminent labour, so as I had a hospital appointment later that morning, Eddie suggested that I should wait until then. As the baby was not due for another two weeks the doctor who saw me said that I was not in labour and should go home. At four o' clock I had terrible backache; my neighbour telephoned for my husband to come home from work, and again I went to the hospital. Again they repeated that the birth was not imminent and sent Eddie home, but this time they let me stay. An hour later Kirsty was born when I was alone in the delivery room. Had I not experienced this overwhelming feeling that my baby would be born that day, she would have been born at home, unattended.

When the girls were small I used to take them out for an afternoon walk past offices which overlooked Church Green in the centre of Redditch. I always felt attracted to those particular buildings, and wished that I could work there. When

Kirsty was four my mother offered to look after the children so that I could return to work, so I registered as a 'temp'. The agency was in one of the offices I so admired, and after a couple of weeks I was asked to call in. I wondered if I had done something wrong, and went in fear and trembling. To my surprise and delight the manageress offered me a position in the agency itself, my wish had been fulfilled.

The manageress and her assistant *Sheila* were both spiritualists and they invited me along to their church. In order not to appear antisocial I went with them. I came out thinking that everyone was mad, and they would never get me there again. The next week however the manageress could not go, and Sheila asked me to go with her. I agreed on the condition that we could go for a drink afterwards!

There were two mediums there that evening, a husband and wife, and it was the wife who had a remarkable message for Sheila. She gave Sheila the name of her brother who had died in a motorcycle accident twenty years previously. She gave many other details, even down to the fact that Sheila had broken the heel of her shoe on the way to church that evening. This certainly opened my eyes, and I began to attend the church more regularly.

My love of books had never left me and I began to read all I could about spiritualism. I went with two friends to the *Spiritualist Association of Great Britain* in London; the search for knowledge was under way! My parents thought that I was insane and kept telling me that I should go to a proper church.

Amongst my readings I had come across an article about the tarot cards which I had found fascinating. The following week I saw a pack in a supermarket of all places; I had no alternative but to buy them. At that time I would not have believed anyone who told me that sometime in the future I would be working professionally with these cards.

I was still sceptical about spiritualism and felt that I needed further proof of its validity. Then at the church one evening a Coventry medium was present. This man, who has now passed on into the spirit world, was in my eyes one of the best mediums I have encountered. That night he came to me and said that he was communicating with a sailor. Canada and Ottawa were mentioned, and also the fact that the sailor was buried at sea with full honours, not drowned as believed. My father-in-law had been in the Royal Navy and died at sea, but we had never been given any details. I knew that *Eddie* had a tin box containing his father's medals, so when I got home I asked him to find it for me. In the box we found a newspaper cutting saying that my father-in-law had received injuries to his stomach and legs, and he had been taken on board a Canadian destroyer. They had been unable to save his life however, and he was buried at sea with full military honours. I was satisfied; I had received the evidence I was looking for.

During the 1979/80 recession the staff agency made severe cut-backs and I was made redundant.This however gave me more time to spend with my mother whose physical condition had been deteriorating for some years. She had been operated on several times for breast cancer, all major operations, and I can remember looking at her during Christmas 1980 and thinking *'You will not be here next Christmas mum'.* During May 1981, on dad's 81st birthday, she was rushed into hospital for yet another operation. It did not go well, and we were told that she only had days, perhaps a week or two to live, and that we could have her back home if we so wished. I am a firm believer that if at all possible we should pass on in our own beds with the people we know and love around us. We arranged for mum to return to her own bungalow. Dad and my aunt were to nurse her during the day, and I was to take over at night.

Mum was quite well for the first two days, but then her condition worsened. Another relative and a friend came to help with the night care, and on the tenth night we were dozing in the lounge when we heard voices coming from mum's room. The door was always ajar so that we could hear her if she needed us. I realized that the others had heard the voices too. The words were indistinct, but we could hear the babble of sound. The three of us pushed the door open, and as we did so the voices stopped. Mum was sleeping peacefully under the influence of her injections. As soon as we came out of the room the voices began again.

In the early hours of the morning mum woke up and said that they had come for her, but that the time was not yet right. In fact she passed on four days later, and during all that time the spirit voices came and went. One night all three of us also heard music.

The day after mum died, I went round to the bungalow to see dad. When I arrived I found him sitting on a chair with his coat on, looking petrified. He told me that she had come for him, and when I asked who, he replied *'Your mum'.* Apparently he had woken at 5.30am to hear his name being called. He then saw mum standing by the bed with a cup of tea in her hand. She looked so real that he was about to take the cup from her, and then realized what was happening. He spoke to her, told her she was dead, and with that she faded through the wall.

I calmed dad down, and he came home with me. Interestingly my daughter asked me who had been lying on nan's bed, the pillow had a definite dent in it as if someone had been lying there.

Within a few days, before mum's cremation I had a dream that I came to a building and knocked on the door. Two ladies dressed like nuns answered, and asked me why mum had passed on. I replied that she had died of cancer. I was told to walk down the corridor and that I would come to a cancer unit. On each side were what seemed like hospital wards with names over them, such as *CANCER, ACCIDENT* and so on. I entered the cancer ward and in a bed beneath a window was my mum. The colours that came through the window and engulfed her were so beautiful, like the rays of a rainbow. Mum looked as fit and well as she had done in her forties. She spoke to me and said that she was waiting for someone. We talked for a little while but then I was told that my time was up. I kissed my mum, said my goodbyes, and returned down the corridor. As the doors opened I woke up. The dream was so vivid, so real with every detail etched in my mind, that I knew it was no normal dream. I believe that in this dreamlike state I went over to the spirit world on to the astral plane. I have had this experience many times since then, and I always write down everything I have encountered when I awake.

Some weeks after mum had died I felt the urge to attend the local spiritualist church. I had not been there for twelve months, and I do not remember much about the service, but do remember staying behind to look at the notice board to see who would be taking the service the following week. Two other ladies were there as well, and of course we started talking. The conversation turned to *tarot cards,* and I mentioned my interest in them. One of the ladies said that she held a small discussion group and healing circle once a week, and invited me to go along. Later that weekend she rang me to ask if I would take my tarot cards along. I nearly had a fit, I had not touched the tarot cards for over twelve months. However I did go and do some short readings for the few people there, and I am pleased to say they made sense to each person. As time went on I was encouraged to do more readings, and I started very slowly to work at one or two psychic fairs. This not only gave me the experience I needed but also opened my eyes to other areas of psychic work, and gave me the opportunity to meet and talk with a variety of people.

I was then asked to give a talk to a Womens' Institute (WI) meeting in a small rural village just outside Redditch. It was to be held in the local anglican church, but the altar had to be blocked off. I was assured that there would be no more than about twenty people present, but when I entered the church I was confronted by about seventy five women, from all walks of life. I had been asked to talk on clairvoyance, tarot cards and my work as a medium, and despite my nerves the evening was a success. This led to many more WI groups contacting me and asking me to give talks.

I have over the years given lectures and held discussion groups with a variety of organisations, including conservative ladies, young farmers, the British Legion, young wives and even a group of personnel managers. My work has taken me all over the midlands region, and it all started with a chance conversation in the spiritualist church. The lady who invited me into her group all those years ago is still a firm friend, despite differences of opinion from time to time. Discussion, agreement, and disagreement form a major part of our spiritual development.

2 Spirit Communication

*M*any *times I am asked how I see spirit. Do I actually see spirit, do I hear it, is there a difference between a medium and a clairvoyant, and if so what is it?*

The word *clairvoyance* comes from the french language and translates as *clear seeing*: *clairaudience* is from the same source and means *clear hearing*.

A clairvoyant can work in many ways, she can use the crystal, the palm, tarot cards, rune stones and even ordinary playing cards. All these methods are ways of opening the psychic channel and projecting into the future.

A clairaudient on the other hand can hear spirit, and is able to relay information from the spirit world.

How do I see spirit? The first signs of paranormal phenomena are tiny dancing lights which form in the space in front of me. The person for whom I am reading will often brush their face as if there were cobwebs on it. As time progresses these lights will form into figures of spirit people, and as these develop I am able to ask for information. I do not ask out aloud, but in my mind.

It is important to realize that entities can manipulate people, and by playing with spiritual circles, evil spirits can be called up instead of good. A true medium will always be in control, and will have asked for guidance and protection from the higher levels of the other world. This is why trance mediumship (see p.16) and deep meditation can be dangerous because the medium may lose control of her own person and become 'possessed' by an evil spirit.

There has been a lot of adverse comment about the *Ouija* board, which was developed in Europe as a board game, the name being derived from the French and German words meaning yes, yes. There is no doubt that in the wrong hands it can attract evil and unwanted entities. Under the control of a good medium however, and under carefully controlled circumstances, the most remarkable links with the other world can be made.

Some years ago I was one of a circle of five who met regularly on a Friday night to use the Ouija board. One evening when I had my finger on the tumbler, it moved and picked out the letters spelling *White Feather*. We asked questions, and were told that when on the earth plane he had been an American Indian. He told us where he came from, but of course this meant nothing to us, although I still have the place written down in my notes. I asked whether I would ever do platform work as a medium, and if so, where? I was told that in the month of August I would be going to a church in Yardley. It was also impressed on me that whenever I did this kind of work I must put my thoughts out to White Feather; I was told that a book would come into my hands which would confirm the White Feather connection.

That Christmas my sister-in-law gave me a book which was called *Strangers who walk amongst us* by Ruth Montgomery, and in one chapter it mentioned group minds and the *White Feather Group*. The Ouija board had come through with remarkable evidence, and this I believe was the link with the wallpaper I had chosen many years previously for my bedroom (see p.8).

I received further evidence when I did start to do some platform work. It was mainly at Redditch Spiritualist Church, but as time went by I was asked to take a service at St. Michael's Healing Sanctuary in Yardley - and the month was August!

My first service will always stand out, because the medium who was due to take the service did not arrive, and I was asked to fill in. As I began to work the messages became stronger, but I learnt that night to give out all that spirit was giving me, and to close myself down completely at the end of the service, for that evening I ended up taking someone home with me. Every message which I gave out was taken, but I had a young man in spirit who had passed over because of a car accident. He was so clear, but I did not know who to go to with him, so I never gave him out.

After the service, my friend and I made our way home, but the car did not behave too well on the journey, and as we stopped outside my friend's house we heard the noises. It seemed as if someone was knocking on the top of the car, and then the noises changed and appeared to be coming from the engine. Mentally I asked who it was, and through clairaudience held a conversation by tapping on the car. I discovered that it was the young man who had contacted me at the church. I told him that I would try to find the person he wanted to get in touch with, but that he had to leave us now. Sadly I was never able to find the contact for him.

This particular friend and I had many memorable experiences together. Another one that stands out in my memory occurred on a Thursday evening. We had decided not to go to church because of the very icy conditions outside. My friend lit the gas fire in her front room, but it was still dreadfully cold and I sat by the fire in my heavy coat trying to get warm. Suddenly the crystal ball that my friend was looking into moved straight across the table; we both jumped back in surprise, and then realized that someone was with us in spirit. I acknowledged him, and said that we hoped to go to church the following Saturday evening and could he then confirm who he was. Suddenly the room became very warm, and we knew the spirit was no longer with us. Saturday came, and we took ourselves off to church. The medium for the evening came straight to us and told us that she had a man with her in spirit who said that we would know who he was because *'everything was as clear as a crystal ball'*. So the spirit who had come to us on Thursday also came through on the Saturday as I had asked.

I remember another remarkable service in 1989. A young man made contact who had passed over when he was shot by the IRA. A neighbour recognised him when he came through with his mother's name, together with the fact that his mother was a seamstress.

Recently I took a service in Leamington Spa and made contact with a lady who had been stabbed to death. I also picked up New Zealand. A man in the congregation said that he understood the message, and at the end of the service he came to me and told me that he was about to return home to New Zealand. He said how pleased he was that he had attended this service before leaving. Later he wrote to me from New Zealand and explained that his son had stabbed his mother, and then tried to kill himself. Although this had been an unsuccessful attempt the lady in spirit was speaking to me about her son and suicide, and I learnt from the father that he did in fact go on to commit this act. I feel that the mother had come through to tell me that she was waiting for her son on the other side.

At some services, names, dates etc. cannot be taken by those present, but I always ask that they enquire amongst their families, and almost always these people come to me at a later date and acknowledge the information that I have given.

3 Working as a Medium

Many people ask me about my religious beliefs, what and who is God, and what is life? These are difficult questions, but I will try to explain my philosophies as I have come to understand them.

I believe that God is a *supreme power* who is both a *creator and an energy force*. We as humans are linked into this energy, and at times we are more aware of this fact than at others. There are many pathways to this supreme energy; some religions imagine God as a mountain up which there are many tracks.

From my *helpers and guides* I am told that over the next few years we shall see the start of a change in religion, which will eventually lead to one single pathway where we can all one day, regardless of colour or creed, work together towards the supreme power of God.

As to the question 'what is life', well everything that exists is life. Every living thing consists of molecules which are in constant vibrating motion. These molecules are very small, but can be seen under a microscope.

Smaller particles known as atoms are also an important constituent of life. An atom is like a miniature solar system and the nucleus of the atom represents the sun in our own solar system.

The development of this concept is very complex, and perhaps all we need to know at this stage is that man is a mass of rapidly rotating molecules. We appear to be solid, but this solidity is an illusion forced on us by our human limitations. Try to imagine how a very small creature, a tiny insect, might see us. Possibly it would see a mass of whirling molecules, which to one so small might appear as many bright lights, just as we with our limited vision see our own stars in the night sky. Try to stretch your mind to the possibilities that I am suggesting.

Each man is a universe in which planets (molecules) spin around a central sun, and every rock, twig or drop of water is composed similarly of molecules in never ending motion. This constant motion generates a form of electricity, which when united with the overself gives life.

I have a theory that when a handicapped child is born, the overself has not fused together perfectly with the electric force, and this causes a malfunction rather like a faulty battery.

No man is a world unto himself; every living thing depends on the existence of other worlds and the intercommunication that exists between them.

This leads me into the area of *ghosts*. A so called ghost has its molecules more widely spaced, so it can easily pass through a brick wall or solid door. Remember that a brick wall is also a collection of molecules suspended in space, which appear solid to us, but is not solid to a ghost or other creatures from the astral planes, known as the *elementaries*. These are in the words of Helena Blavatsky *'souls which for one reason or another have separated from their divine spirits; they are usually a trouble to themselves and to humans'.*

The medium/clairvoyant acts as a link between the different molecular structures, or to put it another way, the living and what we would call the dead. Using telepathy, she is able to contact this power of consciousness, where past, present and future can be perceived.

There are many different types of medium; some receive impressions, some can hear and see spirit and even have the ability to produce voices. There is also the trance medium where the 'spirit' enters the body of the medium, and talks through her. Mediums are the receivers, they are like radios, and through their altered state of consciousness, atune themselves with their inspirers and guides.

In what the Spiritualist Movement calls the spirit world there are *helpers, guides, doorkeepers, masters and adepts.* The helpers and guides work with the mediums, and make the bridge between this world and the next. These can range from the Great White Brotherhood to people who have passed over, but chosen to work on the next levels with the medium to whom they are suited. Once a medium has learnt who is with her she must rely on these helpers and guides to be the doorkeepers who will keep away evil or unwanted spirits and only allow the true communicators to be near.

Who then are the masters? Those of us who believe in reincarnation, (a chapter is devoted to this subject later in the book), will know that here on the earth plane humanity consists of men at various stages of spiritual development. A point is reached when men through many incarnations perfect themselves to the stage where they are called *masters.*

In all religions there are the representatives of God himself. The Hindus, whose religion spread in the east, have their great *Avataras* and the *Lord Buddha* while in the western world, Christianity has the master *Jesus*, the Christ himself. These masters are part of the Great White Brotherhood, and I refer to them as the *elders.* They are working both in the astral realms and the physical.

Adepts are workers who are not quite at the level of the masters, but nevertheless give a great deal of help and guidance to us on the earth plane.

At this point I think that I should explain the difference between spiritual communications and thought forms that can be projected. Once a medium has established a link with her sitter, she can often provide names, numbers, dates which the sitter can recognise. This does not in itself provide survival evidence; what it does prove is the power of the mind, and the thoughts, usually subconscious, in the mind of the sitter being picked up by the medium using her psychic channels. This is the use of thought form, and is different to the information given to us directly by spirit, but is just as important and useful.

We should however acknowledge the difference.

Each person has a psychic channel, but in many cases is not aware of its existence; however regrettably, awareness can easily lead to use of the channel for the wrong reasons.

Once the spiritual doorway is open there are dangers that all must be aware of, both on the physical and mental level. A medium must always be aware of these dangers, and be in control of her inner self. She must always acknowledge that group of world services on the other side who are ready to move her thoughts and feelings. She must learn to live as she teaches and keep her spiritual values clear, knowing that she will never stop learning, and by reaching out to that higher self will expand the inner consciousness. She must be careful not to let her mental and physical health wane; both meditation and careful eating are essential.

The less involved a spiritual worker is, the more trials and errors are ahead of her, and if the lines of service are not kept clear there may be a temptation to move into other areas which are not for her. Working mediums must strive to the highest goal, guard against self illusion and not allow the ego to take over. The work and goal in their life must be for spirit and not themselves.

Mediums who are working on the highest levels chose the spiritual pathway before they re-entered the earth plane.

We must never forget that through willingness to serve, a link will be forged with the adepts and masters, which will lead to our own admission into the Great White Brotherhood. Only by working in service with God, and realizing that God is love can progression of any kind be made. Often the work takes many life times, and many years in each life time, and only when one has reached a certain level, can the mental planes be reached, and contact made with the elders. Many times we will be put to the test, and many times we will fail; we must never give in, but continue to serve and be constant in our endeavour.

4 Is there Life after Death?

*I*s death the end? I am asked this so many times and my answer is simply 'No'!

When we make the transition which we call death, it is onto another plane, another dimension, much like going to sleep. We do not fear sleep, so why fear death?

The only certain thing that anyone can predict is that we will all make this transition one day through the gate marked death. Only God knows when that day will be. Yet this is an event which the majority of humans refuse to think about or face up to until it touches their personal life. If we were making a journey to another part of the country, most of us would attempt to familiarise ourselves with the route, consult a map and generally prepare ourselves, but for this ultimate journey many are unwilling to discuss or even acknowledge it, so that when the time comes they are caught unawares.

Many people fear existence after death. Often this is because of the urge to cling to the body and the material side of life, or it is possible they have a subconscious memory of a former death. However for the spiritually minded person and the highly evolved spirit, death is a release of the spirit to a better world.

When we are faced with the death of one we love, we should realize that what is occurring is the astral birth into a new and better place. Initially we should not hold or move the body to allow the transition to occur easily. We should send our loved one onto the next plane with prayers and love, and should try very hard to avoid despair and sorrow, for such vibrations could slow down this transition period. We should remember that all sorrow is for our own loss, and as such is an act of selfishness. Of course we will be sad, but if we understand that wishing them to be with us is hindering their spiritual progress; if we truly love them we should let them go, gladly.

It is also important that at the moment of death no-one who is unsympathetic to the deceased is in the same room, for the astral birth may be hampered by the vibrations of that person.

I often smile when I am asked, as I frequently am, what happens when we die and meet someone on the other side who we did not get on with over here. If you were totally incompatible in this life, then you will not meet on any other plane of existence. This applies to husbands, wives and any other relationship. It is interesting to note that you may have had a lesson to learn, which is the reason why your life had to become entwined with theirs on this plane.

Over the next few decades the development of the psychic energy within the human race will create the power of the physical eye to reveal the *etheric body* (see next paragraph), and we will all be able to see and communicate with our loved ones who have gone that little way ahead. There will not be the need for mediums, psychics or clairvoyants as we know them. There will be teachers coming onto this earth plane to show people how to use this thought communication link. Religion as we know it will disappear and when the time is right the psychic and spiritual centres will appear, and the words of one of our great masters, Jesus, who said that we are all sons of God, will have more meaning. My guides have given me the information that teachers have already arrived on this earth plane, but work in their own way to open the human mind. When one day we are more highly developed, we will be able to read each others minds, and be able to lead the ones with dark thoughts onto the pathway of light, and on towards the Godhead.

Let me explain what I mean by the etheric body, which I mentioned earlier. This relates to the magnetic field which surrounds the human body. The etheric covers the body, and extends for about an eighth of an inch round each part of the body, even each strand of hair. With a little patience most people are able to see the etheric body, and with even more patience and practice, the aura can be seen as well. What you will see is a slight mist rising from the body.

Sometimes people who think they have seen a ghost, have actually seen the etheric or energy field of someone who once existed on the earth plane. An etheric body can often be seen moving away from a newly departed body for several days. People often say that they have seen mist rising from new graves in cemeteries, and this has given rise to many ghost stories. I understand that it is better to be cremated than buried, because this frees the etheric body and the spirit more quickly.

The subject of death or transition is one that many psychics and mediums have written about, some more successfully than others. As with all my writings I have communicated information as it has been given to me by my guides, although even so I do not know the answers to all the questions.

5 Karma and Reincarnation

Karma is a term derived from the Sanskrit root kri ('to do' or 'to make'), and should be interpreted to mean action. It can loosely be described as the law of consequences, 'as you sow, so shall you reap'. It can be regarded as the fruits of action in one lifetime determining the conditions of a life in future incarnations.

The operation of Karma in the words of the great theosophist Annie Besant (1847-1933) is set out as follows:- *'the desire to do a thing in one life usually precipitates itself as a compulsion and capacity to act out that desire in a subsequent life. Repeated thoughts in one life precipitate as a distinct tendency in a later life, while the will to perform certain acts will become transformed into actual ability to perform them in a later life'.*

There is no doubt in my mind that our lives are one continuous flow, and as we pass from one body to another we are learning and working out a plan for our future lives. We are also paying for past weakness and immorality.

The law of Karma and rebirth makes sense of life itself, it makes life purposeful and enables us to create our own destiny. We must never forget that we are given a choice, our free will, to decide how our lives develop and progress. No life is ever wasted; in every thought and action we are learning and growing in experience.

The frequency of rebirth depends on many things; the spiritual level attained by the soul, the number of years lived in each life, and the intended aims of that soul. An ordinary human may possibly only reincarnate once every 700 to 800 years, whereas one who has reached a high level of purity would be free to reincarnate almost immediately if this was necessary to achieve his spiritual purpose.

Not everyone is prepared to believe in reincarnation, but more and more people are opening their minds to this way of thinking. An inner awareness of life on this planet can lead to the realization that we are makers of our own destiny, and that we choose our tomorrow. We are sowing the seeds to gather a harvest, good or bad, and maybe the reaping will not be in this life but the next. Every act is a seed planted and a harvest to be gathered.

Let me enlarge a little more on the belief in reincarnation. The belief is at its strongest in *Hinduism,* where the soul is considered to be a deep reflection of the one soul, and the goal of each person's whole existence is to become one with *Brahma,* the divine. Before going on to attain this unity, the soul must reincarnate many times, both as animals and humans. The whole cycle of this wheel of rebirth is known to them as Sansara, it is like the universe itself.

To the western mind it is seen more as 'survival' of the soul, working off a karmic debt. If we look at this idea more carefully we will recognise that the way we live today, the place we live and who are parents are, were all to some extent chosen before we entered this earth plane as a direct result of what has gone before. I have a strong feeling that before our rebirth we are given the opportunity to witness the life we will lead before we enter the physical body. It is often said that a drowning man sees the whole of his life flash before him. Maybe the same thing happens in reverse.

How many times do we think that we have done things previously? It could be that we have brought with us memories of a past life, or that we have witnessed the scene in the *akashic records*. These are historical records of all world events and personal experiences of all thoughts and actions, which have taken place on the earth, and may in normal circumstances only be read by the adepts. Mediums however through their guides are sometimes privileged to have access to these records.

The power of thought cannot be over stressed. We must realize that thought is energy and energy is thought, so we can in a way create what we say and do. We know the power of positive and negative thought; positive thinking leading to success and achievement, negative thought to all manner of ills. The apostle Paul said '*as a man thinketh, so is he*'.

We must start living every minute of the day, and not let the past affect our future. Instead we must let our energy affect our future, affect the person we are, how we think and what we say. We must realize that in everything we do we are building our future life pattern. Our thoughts are seeds of energy and growth, and by getting rid of past negativity we are pulling weeds out of the new seeds of growth. This will make our life stronger and more positive, and ensure we look beyond this life to the next.

We should always watch how our actions reflect on others; we should not do anything to hurt or harm anyone, and we should willingly help others without reflecting what is in it for us. *As we give so shall we receive.* This is a very true statement.

Our lives are like a tapestry which does not make a picture until it is fully woven, but when the weaving is finished the scene is wonderful. We are also a part of the greater tapestry of life, within which we all have a pathway to follow, some the warp and some the weft. We are all at different levels of life, but each is something special and necessary to the whole; whether good or bad we are part of the creation.

Belief in reincarnation helps the progression of the soul, but I understand that many people find it hard to accept. Indeed some spiritualists have not yet come to a clear conclusion about this life. Some believe that there are various planes or spheres which they go on to, and they also think that there is spiritual progression open to every soul, but many draw the line at rebirth. They are only interested in survival and progression of the soul at the astral level.

Many people have gone back to past lives through hypnotic regression, and many young children have amazed adults with memories of happenings which could only relate to a previous lifetime. I firmly believe that the ancient law of Karma does exist, and I say again to each of you who reads this book, *'OPEN YOUR MIND AND EXPLORE'!*

Is it not heartening to know that all our life is a constant learning, developing experience, built on experiences and knowledge gained in previous lives? Does it not give us a reason for living, to progress, to serve, to open our minds to find our ultimate purpose? Does it not remove any fear of death, and help us see it only as the next major step in our spiritual progress?

6 Colours of the Aura

Just as the etheric body is an energy field surrounding the human body, so too is the aura, and as I have said previously, with practice and patience, it can be seen by the human eye. The etheric and aura are enclosed together in a sheath completely surrounding the human body.

Within the aura are colours, which reflect the spirituality, personality and health of the person. It shows moods, thoughts, love and sickness. If a person is very ill the aura fades over a period of time, and occasionally fades completely before they die, leaving only the etheric. At other times, perhaps if someone is killed accidentally, the aura will remain for some moments after death.

Often it is difficult to believe in things which we are told are part of us, and yet we can neither feel nor see. Yet we cannot see the air we breathe, unless we exhale it from our lungs on a cold and frosty day. So too under certain circumstances and with practice, does the aura become visible and maybe even then only to those sensitive enough to perfect the art. However, anyone with any degree of sensitivity can sense an aura, even if they cannot see it.

For those able to see, the aura consists of several colours, and it is worth noting that the wearing of certain colours can influence the health, thoughts and life patterns of the wearer. Colours are merely names for various vibrations which enter the earth's aura, and in turn the human aura. Colours of the universe are like musical notes, a combination of vibrations, which need to be compatible with each other. Any lack of compatibility will cause bad vibrations.

As a person progresses on his or her spiritual pathway, the colours in their aura will alter. These colours which pour out of the aura are as those in the rainbow and equally as beautiful. It is interesting to note that the wearing of semi-precious stones in various colours can balance the energy field (aura) around the wearer, and I will be dealing with stones and crystals in a later chapter.

Let us look at the basic common colours seen in auras and the message they communicate.

RED: This colour signifies many things, some rather conflicting. It can mean a driving force, which is why many soldiers and Generals have red in their aura, and in their uniforms, but a rather dark, or muddy red can indicate a moody bad tempered person. A bright scarlet often indicates a person who is unsure of themselves, and can also indicate false pride.

ORANGE: Basically this is a good colour and shows self control. A brownish orange indicates a lazy person.

YELLOW: A golden yellow shows that the possessor is of a most spiritual nature. Note that all saints are depicted with golden haloes. Although it is a most spiritual colour, it is interesting that a very dark yellow can indicate cowardice, and people possessing this colour indicate no knowledge of spiritual progress. Yet we must all have yellow in our aura before we can progress further along the spiritual pathway.

GREEN: This colour is often seen as one of bad luck, and yet this could not be further from the truth. Green is the colour of healing and of teaching. Doctors' have green in their auras, and it is interesting that they wear green gowns in the operating theatre. We speak of people having 'green fingers'; they have a love of plants which thrive under their care, and usually they too will have green in their auras. It seems that unconsciously we are aware of the colours affecting us, and reflect it in the colours we wear and the terminology we use.

BLUE: This is the colour of the spiritual world. It shows intellectual ability apart from the spiritual. As always though, the varying shades have various meanings. A very dark blue will be in the aura of a person with a calling towards God. Pale blue can indicate indecision.

PURPLE/VIOLET: This colour in the aura usually indicates a very religious person. This is why members of the church wear purple in their attire. It is worth mentioning that people with purple in their aura can suffer from stomach disorders and heart trouble.

It is possible for someone who has progressed to an advanced level of mediumship to look at a person's aura, and know what they have been in their past lives, and also to see what lies ahead of them. A medium picking up this information can transfer it to the subject concerned, only if the knowledge would serve their advancement.

One further point about the aura; often we are aware of young people going around in crowds, gangs, call it what you will, but the reason for their clinging together is the sameness of their vibrations. Their auras, acting like magnets are linking together and cause a huge energy field; the young people concerned are out of control and unable to act on their own initiative. Their self discipline needs training, to help them pull out of this energy field, and not go along with the crowd so that they can become their own person and therefore develop their own individuality.

Finally let us remember that pure energy cannot be destroyed, and can be used both positively and negatively; it is the essence of life itself.

7 Psychic and Spiritual Experiences.

*R*eaders *may be interested to know what form my work can take, apart from lecturing and giving sittings.*

I am considered to be a psychic consultant, and this involves me in being called out to houses that are haunted. In some cases I find a situation that just needs calming down; for example a spirit not long passed, may well be trying to prove their survival to loved ones. Recognition of the cause, and acknowledgement of the spirit will stop the activity, and all will be well. In other cases the spirit entities need to be contacted because they are trapped for one reason or another in this earthly existence, and need freeing to continue their journey onto the other side.

Some years ago I was asked to go to a cottage in Droitwich where the family were experiencing much paranormal phenomena. The husband for example, had been locked in the cellar, and the boys had seen a man in their bedroom. Through clairvoyance I was eventually able to discover that the cause of the problem was a previous owner of the cottage who had passed over very suddenly from a heart attack. The situation once understood was calmed down, and the spirit was helped to continue its progress onto the astral level. All paranormal activity then ceased.

On another occasion I was asked to go to a public house. A male ghost had been seen in one of the areas, and was disturbing the lady who ran the pub. Customers standing at the bar had also witnessed the visitor, and the landlady's son also claimed that the ghost had actually spoken to him before suddenly disappearing.

When I entered the public house and tuned in to the vibrations, I was certain that the ghost was someone connected with the landlady, rather than with the building. Through clairaudience I was able to give her a name which she immediately recognised. It was an uncle of whom she had been particularly fond, and on learning that this was who was with her she felt much happier, no longer anxious or disconcerted. I do not know whether he has returned since to visit his niece, but if he has I am sure he would be welcome.

I was asked by a local newspaper to spend two nights in a shopping precinct when security guards had reported that they thought the site was haunted. As a direct result of this report by the security guards, many people had written to the paper relating their own experiences in the centre. A male cleaner had been pushing his machine down a corridor when he saw something white coming out through his machine; this had frightened him sufficiently to cause him to run out of the precinct. A number of people including a security guard, reported seeing a monk, and others had heard a child crying when the centre had been closed at night. Another cleaner had found huge heavy plant containers overturned and all contents spilled only minutes after cleaning the area. A childrens' roundabout, awaiting collection, was discovered by guards to be working, and yet it was not connected to the electricity supply. Unexplained happenings, reported by the staff, had occurred frequently in a store room belonging to one of the multiples.

This was the kind if information I was armed with when I agreed to spend some time in the shopping precinct after it was closed for the night. It was not an altogether pleasant experience; I was acutely aware that there was undoubtedly much paranormal activity in the area. On researching the background I discovered that in order to build this new precinct, churches had been demolished, and many old buildings and tombstones had been built over, and were actually beneath some of the shops. Not that this is necessarily the reason for the activity, but it could certainly have a bearing on it. I was very concerned at the time, because one shop that was built over the graveyard, organised a 'psychic sleep-in' for charity. I warned them of the dangers, but they went ahead, and I have since had calls for help from people who participated and have become very distressed by the experience.

On another occasion I was asked to visit a restaurant where staff had heard their names called, and had been tapped on the shoulder by an unseen hand. Glasses too had been smashed in an abnormal manner. I agreed to visit, and as soon as I reached the main function room I felt as if I wanted to put on a nurse's uniform, and I felt the presence of a man in a wheelchair with his left leg missing. A friend, also a psychic, who had come with me said that he felt the area was unusually cold, and that he was sure that we would find a photograph that would be meaningful to us. We asked the manager if there were any old photographs around and he took us to a part of the restaurant that had been redecorated in 1920s style, and on the wall were photographs of the building and its occupants during that period. I was immediately guided to one particular photograph. It showed a nurse pushing a man in a wheelchair; he had one leg missing. We were told that the building had served as a hospital during the First World War, and we knew that we had identified our ghost. Far from being terrified, the manager and staff told us that it was nice to know who was responsible for the hauntings, and the atmosphere became comfortable for them all again.

Sometimes when I visit homes where psychic activity has been experienced I discover that someone in the family is a natural sensitive without them realizing it, that is, a person who is able to create energy which somebody from the other side is able to use. They are therefore creating a channel for psychic experiences to occur. Children are often natural sensitives, and sometimes things can get out of control. Part of my job is to go in and take control of the situation, and for this you do have to be very strong and stand firm. Doubt, fear, uncertainty will only serve to increase the unwelcome activity. Never once must you doubt the ability of your helpers to persuade this often disruptive element to move on.

Cases of this type are not pleasant to experience, because you can feel very threatened, and must stand your ground. I was called out to a farm where they were experiencing very strange happenings. I was taken to one particular barn which could no longer be put to any useful purpose because heavy objects needing two or three men to move, were being displaced constantly, and would never stay where they were put. As we walked towards the barn, the two dogs that were with us skirted all the way round it, and would not rejoin us until we had left the area. Inside the barn the atmosphere was unpleasant, and suddenly the alarm went off. The farmer took me to look at the alarm bell that had just been triggered; the wires had been cut and the alarm disconnected, but he told me this alarm was always going off.

The farmer's sister who had previously occupied a bungalow on the farm told me that she had seen a tall cloaked 'figure' entering her home. The house, she said, was always very cold. I learned that ten acres of the land had previously been forest land and that many old trees had been cut down to build barns for livestock. I felt that this had disturbed something in the land which was causing the paranormal activity. I was very pleased to leave the place, and then was horrified to learn that thirty hours after my visit an unexplained fire had broken out in the barn exactly on the spot on which I had stood. Offices and a warehouse had been destroyed, and although the police and insurance company put the fire down to arson, no one was arrested, and no explanation or reason could be found. I am quite sure that on that farm there was so much psychic energy present, that my visit acted like a match, I had certainly been made aware that whatever it was did not want me there. We often talk about igniting situations, this time I'm sure I did! I must add that both the police and the insurance company were informed of my visit.

A few months ago I was asked to go into an old house which had been bought by the Regional Health Authority. Part of it was being used as offices and part of it for rehabilitation of people with psychiatric disorders prior to their return into the community. Both day and night staff had reported phenomena. I stayed on the premises for a while and asked through prayer that the situation be eased. I talked to the staff, and tried to calm their fears.

I heard later that although the experiences were continuing, the people living there were not being quite as disturbed, and were able to sleep at night. However they asked me to return and work again on the phenomena. This I agreed to do, but half an hour before I was due to leave to keep my appointment I received a telephone call cancelling the visit. The Health Authority did not want me to return, because they distrusted my work. It is such a pity that people do not understand the nature of what I do, and realize that far from being harmful, it is a force for good, and can give so much help to people in need.

While we are on the subject of paranormal experiences, it might interest readers to hear of other people's experiences as they have been told to me. People often come to talk to me about things that have happened to them, often because they need reassurance; they have tried to relate their experience to others and have either been laughed at or looked at in a strange way. As one lady put it, *'I began to think people thought I was a candidate for the men in white coats, in fact I began to think I was too'*. People need to be reassured that what they have 'seen' or experienced is not an uncommon occurrence, and they are not going mad.

A lady from Worcester who was a delivery driver was out on her rounds in the country, when she drove past an old lady, laden with shopping, standing by the side of the road. She stopped and asked the lady if she would like a lift. The old lady replied that she was most grateful, but that she was going in the opposite direction. The delivery driver said she did not mind turning round and giving her a lift, so the old lady got into the van and explained where she wanted to go, saying that she wanted to be dropped off at some crossroads.

Eventually they arrived at the crossroads, and as the old lady thanked the driver, she put her hand on her knee - it felt icy cold. She clambered out of the van and said goodbye. The van driver then turned her vehicle round, and returned the way she had come, arriving a few minutes later at the spot where she had picked up the old lady. She was very shocked to see standing in exactly the same place, the lady laden with her shopping. There was no way she could have walked back there in the time it had taken the van to reach the spot. Needless to say, she did not stop a second time, and the speedometer clocked a few extra mph as she sped away from the scene.

A young man I met told me that one evening about six o' clock he was out with some friends, when a man suddenly walked in front of his car. They all felt the man hit the car, go over the top, and appear to fall on the road. In a panic they stopped and got out of the car, but there was no one to be seen. They looked all around, in a ditch beside the road, anywhere the man could have been thrown, but there was no sight of him. They drove to the local police station to report the incident, and the response from the policeman on duty was *'Oh dear, not again!'* Apparently a man had been killed some years before at that spot, and every now and then he reappeared to re-enact the accident. I do have an explanation for this; when someone is killed violently, for example murdered or in an accident, this seems to leave an impression on time. It is as if this impression has been recorded and from time to time in the future someone is able to tap into this recorded impression.

Another incident told to me was by a lady who was brought up in a cottage on a large estate. Her father was the gamekeeper. One day while out on his rounds he was walking across a bridge when he felt a breeze behind him. He turned to see a hooded figure approaching. The figure glided past at quite a speed and as it did so the gamekeeper was hardly able to breathe for the stench. Although the day was calm the leaves began to rustle and the trees swayed. Shortly afterwards the gamekeeper left his position on the estate, but he took a photograph of his cottage as a momento. When the film was a developed, a figure could be clearly seen in the window of the empty cottage, waving to him.

I heard of the following experiences when I gave a talk to a group of business people in Wales.

A lady and her husband bought a piece of land and had a house built. The day the moved in, all went well. They retired to bed but about 3am they heard a child crying. They searched the house high and low but could not find anything. The crying continued until about 4.30am when it stopped. The following night the same thing occurred, so the next day they visited the local priest who was unable to help, but directed them to the local council to find out the previous history of the land. They discovered that many years before, a house had stood on the same site, and in it a child had been murdered. The house had eventually been pulled down and the land left undeveloped until the couple had bought it. They decided to have the house blessed, and the crying stopped.

Another lady told me about her baby boy. One evening when the child was about nine months old, they heard a noise in his bedroom. They went to investigate and found their son apparently fast asleep but speaking like an adult in a strange tongue, which sounded to be Latin. They were completely taken aback, but had the presence of mind to start praying. The boy stopped and they have never experienced anything similar again.

There is no doubt that many children have psychic experiences, and there have been many remarkable events concerning children. How many times have we seen our own children playing with what we have called 'imaginary' friends. How many times have we told them that there isn't really anybody there. Childrens lack of inhibition makes them more aware and open to psychic experiences, which more often than not they accept as normal. It is only as they grow and take on the conventions and limitations of society, that their minds start to close down and their awareness of 'things beyond' is lost. We need to be aware again as a child; all of us still have this psychic ability, but most have simply lost the art of using it.

8 The Zodiac and The New Age

*A*s *the New Age of Aquarius dawns, a new interest in astrology will emerge, and the great store of knowledge within the cosmos will be unlocked to those who search for the key (cosmos comes from the greek word for order).*

The signs of Aries and Libra represent within the cosmos the Father and the Son. The *Zodiac* is like a book in which we will find, if we study well, through symbolism it reveals the destiny of man and the universe. By understanding the Zodiac we will be lead into some secrets of the Godhead itself. We must remember however that we cannot in one life know everything; it may take several lives.

Most of us are familiar with the twelve signs of the Zodiac; *Aquarius, Pisces, Aries, Taurus, Gemini, Cancer, Leo, Virgo, Libra, Scorpio, Sagittarius, Capricorn,* all of which are symbolised by animals. Hopefully we may also be familiar with the seven planets, *Sun, Moon, Mars, Mercury, Venus, Jupiter, and Saturn,* the seven days of the week are named after these planets, starting with the sun and moon, sunday and monday.

In the western world the life force is seen as the four elements, *fire, earth, air and water,* and within these elements are fixed the associated astrological signs, along with the planets; colours and numbers are also associated with these elements. Here are the four elements with some of their components.

FIRE
Astrological signs: Aries, Leo, Sagittarius.
Colours: gold, orange, red.
Planets: Sun, Mars, Jupiter.
Numbers: 1, 3, 4, 9.

EARTH
Astrological signs: Capricorn, Taurus, Virgo.
Colours: black, brown, green, white.
Planets: Saturn, Venus.
Numbers: 5, 6, 8.

AIR
Astrological signs: Aquarius, Gemini, Libra.
Colours: blue-white, white, yellow.
Planets: Saturn, Venus.
Numbers: 4, 5, 6.

WATER
Astrological signs: Cancer, Pisces, Scorpio.
Colours: blue, green, grey.
Planets: Moon, Neptune.
Numbers: 2, 3, 7, 9.

It is interesting to know that the symbolism of the Zodiac is written in to stories within the Bible. A study of *Revelations Chapter 5* will reveal that the seven spirits of God are mentioned (the planets). There are also four beasts, the first like a lion (leo), the second a calf (taurus), the third a man (aquarius), the fourth an eagle (scorpio), although the scorpion is now the commonly used symbol for scorpio. There are many more instances, but this would take another book to refer to and explain them all.

There is no doubt that a plan lies ahead for mankind which is out of our hands, and we are at the beginning of this marvellous new age which will open the spiritual realism of God's Kingdom for man. If you wish to develop your awareness of this new age, I suggest you read some books about the *Essenes*, whose teachings I believe, are coming to the fore at this time for a reason. Their teachings will lead the minds of men forward into the Age of Aquarius. Jesus, when he was preparing for his ministry, was taught by the Essenes; they were a sect who lived by the shores of the Dead Sea, 2,000 years ago, and were responsible for the *Dead Sea Scrolls.*

We are now leaving the old ways behind and are preparing for the birth of the new age. We are being exposed to change, and we only need to look around our world today to see the enormous changes that have occurred already. Those yet to come will surprise us all, unless of course we are prepared. Although we still have twenty four hours in a day, time seems to be speeding up. There does not appear to be enough time in a day, week or year. Children seem to be born at a more advanced stage of development than children of a few years ago. They are more 'knowing', appear to communicate earlier and mature sooner. I have no doubt that this is part of the plan for mankind by the Great Being, within which we live and have our own being.

When we start on the pathway of esoteric studying, we realize that laws are controlled by a cosmic law which is made by God. Laws made by man are there to keep society in order. There are often differences between God's law and man's law; for instance, in the Bible the future was predicted many times, even by Jesus himself, but in man's law in Britain it is illegal to predict the future under the *Fraudulent Mediums Act* which replaced the old *Witchcraft Act.* wIt is worth thinking deeply about this, and considering other areas where the law of man and the law of God may differ.

Finally to return to the Zodiac, knowing the time, date and place of birth, and understanding all the implications of the positions of planets and signs in a horoscope at the moment of birth will indicate the best pathways to take through this life, without removing the gift of free will. All this has little to do with the horoscopes we read in the morning papers, but which is how so many people think of astrology. At the end of this book I have made suggestions for further reading which you should find useful if you wish to follow this particular path towards spiritual development.

9 The Tarot

The Tarot is a pack of cards, which is related to the ordinary modern day playing cards. The cards are widely used for fortune telling and mystical purposes, and when used properly are capable of very deep mystical understanding, although in parts of Europe it is played purely as a 'parlour game'.

No one is quite sure of their origin, but it seems that the word tarot has been derived from Egyptian, Hebrew or Latin, and could have come from *Astaroth,* the Goddess of fertility of Syria and Palestine. This Goddess was condemned in the Old Testament for the sensuality of her rites.

Whatever their derivation, they hold certain mysteries which are a mixed association of mythology, legend and magic, and seem to hold a key to the mysteries of life. It is said that if a person were imprisoned with nothing but the tarot, they would acquire universal knowledge over a period of years.

Early accounts of their use go back to 1392 or earlier, when a monk called Brother John wrote an essay about them in Switzerland. Certainly Charles VI of France had a pack designed and made for himself, and in the Bibliotheque Nationale of Paris there are seventeen cards said to have belonged to the King.

I use three different packs of tarot cards, *the Swiss Tarot, the Wirth Tarot* and the *Rider-Waite Tarot. Wirth* was a practitioner of magnetism; he was a freemason and a member of the French Theosophical Society which had been founded by the remarkable *Madame Helena Blavatsky* in New York in 1875, her aim being to build a bridge between religion, science and eastern traditions. *A.E.Waite* designed and wrote many books on the tarot. He was born in 1857 and died in the London blitz in 1940. He was a believer in tradition and his books covered areas of freemasonry, rosicrucianism, ceremonial magic and the Grail legends. He too was involved with the Theosophical Society and spiritualism. In the year 1910 he published with Pamela Colman Smith the book *Key to the Tarot* and they jointly designed the pack known as the *Rider-Waite tarot*. This was to become the most well known tarot pack and continues to be available for purchase.

I personally have a great feeling for the tarot cards, and for me they disclose many secrets, but I know that this is not the case for everyone, only for those who are drawn to it. Many others are finding their own pathway to the inner knowledge of self and spiritual enlightenment. For me however the tarot is like the tree of life itself with many branches through which to climb. These branches entwine with the hebrew alphabet, and have a hidden system which brings together the planets, signs of the zodiac, animals, plants and precious stones. It is like a book of creation.

There is a book of creation which was written in hebrew sometime between the third and sixth century AD, called the *Sefa Jetsiral*. It was translated into Latin about the year 1552 and published in Paris. Information contained in this book intimated that it held the key, and that 'God' engraved his name and manifested his identity throughout the universe through expressions of numbers, letters and sounds. There can be no doubt that the symbols and signs on the tarot cards relate to the history and all the phenomena of the universe and the one God. By studying the tarot in depth it is possible to link the sayings and pictures to quotations from the bible.

The tarot pack consists of a deck of 78 cards; it can be used to predict trends in life, and with understanding provides the key to the secrets of the universe. Of the 78 cards, 22 are picture cards and are known as the *Major Arcana,* the remaining 56 being the *Minor Arcana*. The pictures of the major arcana are of a deeply symbolic nature in which colours, forms and illustrations combine to stimulate the mind of the person using the cards. The 56 cards of the minor arcana symbolise the four elements of the earth, and the cards themselves resemble ordinary playing cards.

Below are listed the 22 major arcana cards along with their astrological influences. The 22 cards are associated with the 22 letters of the Hebrew alphabet and the 22 pathways of the tree of life.

Paths	Major Arcana	Hebrew	Planets
1	0 Fool	Aleph	Air
2	1 Magician	Baeth	Mercury
3	2 High Priestess	Gimel	Moon
4	3 Empress	Batetch	Venus
5	4 Emperor	Che	Aries
6	5 Pope	Vall	Taurus
7	6 Lovers	Zain	Gemini
8	7 Chariot	Heth	Cancer
9	8 Strength	Teth	Leo
10	9 Hermit	God	Virgo
11	10 Wheel of Fortune	Kaph	Jupiter
12	11 Justice	Hames	Libra
13	12 Hangman	Mem	Water
14	13 Death	Nun	Scorpio
15	14 Temperance	Samekl	Sagittarius
16	15 Devil	Agin	Capricorn
17	16 Tower	Pie	Mars
18	17 Star	Tzaddi	Aquarius
19	18 Moon	Qopit	Pisces
20	19 Sun	Resh	Sun
21	20 Judgement	Shim	Fire
22	21 World	Tau	Saturn

Let me give you an example of the use of the tarot, using the ten card spread. A lady came to me concerned about her relationships, and where this side of her life was leading. I worked with the Major Arcana, and the first card she turned up was the Emperor. This card represents a man sitting on a cubic throne; this indicated to me that there was a man around her who wanted power over her. This was crossed by the Death card which was symbolic of a change of direction and followed again by the card representing the 'door of the sanctuary', the second card in the pack; this indicated that the lady was looking for peace of mind and she needed to go into her inner self for direction.

The next card was the Tower, indicating destruction, which to me indicated the need to let go of the material bond tying her to this man, an unavoidable parting which was meant to be. This was followed by the eleventh card, which represents Leo and strength, showing that she would have the strength to pull away from the situation, and that she must have faith in herself. The card to follow was the twelfth arcana, the Hangman, which represents sacrifice. My interpretation was that she would need to be prepared to sacrifice some material wealth in order to gain this peace of mind.

The fourteenth card that followed represented harmony and meant that she was moving into a better period, but would require patience. Next came the eighth arcana bringing justice and balance to the situation around her. The seventh card followed, meaning the conqueror or victory, represented by the Gemini sign and indicating that good would overcome, and the situation would all come together. This was followed by the nineteenth arcana the Sun and the sign of the fishes, meaning the emergence from darkness into light and the ultimate truth.

The final card was the Wheel of Fortune meaning to know, to will, to strive upwards, to leave behind the darkness and to look ahead to new beginnings. The summary of all this was that she would need to make some important decisions, but would have the strength to carry through any decision that she made. This would mean a sacrifice, but her peace of mind and a new beginning were available to her if she strove upwards and towards the light.

Of course the lady had the freedom of will to either take note of the indications in the cards and act on them, or go away and forget about it all, but she had asked for help and the cards had shown a way. Never forget that we all have the freedom of choice in whatever decision we make or pathway we choose, and that choice is our responsibility alone.

The interpretation of this spread will I hope give an idea of how the tarot cards work. Do remember that a great deal depends on the vibrations of the person reading, and indeed on the sitter. Another person with similar cards would not have an identical reading.

If you feel that you must have a pack of cards, please respect them. Look after them and above all spiritually understand them for they hold many mysteries. They can unfold the spiritual inner self and set it on a wonderful pathway to adventure.

10 Gemstones and Crystals

***People** over the ages have been using gemstones for spiritual growth and healing. I have no doubt that the ability to work with and understand these stones and crystals helps to develop the spiritual side of life.*

Gemstones were important in biblical times. There is much occult and ancient wisdom and philosophy attached to the stones. For example, in *Exodus Chapter 28* verse 17, the bible states that in the breastplate of judgement there will be four rows of stones, which are as follows: First row *sardius, topaz* and *carbuncle.* Second row *emerald, sapphire and diamond.* Third row *ligure, agate and amethyst.* Fourth row *beryl, onyx and jasper,* all to be set in gold. It goes on to say that the stones shall be with the names of the children of Israel, and should be worn on the breastplate next to the heart when going into a holy place.

There are some variations in the names of the gems in the breastplate, depending on the ancient authority writing the account. For example what is an *agate* in the revised version of the Bible in 1884 AD, is called *achates* in the Vulgate (Latin) about 400 AD. In Josephus (Greek) about 90 AD it is *amethystos*, in Septuagint (Greek) about 250 BC *achates* and in Hebrew *shebo*.

High priests wore twelve stones in their vestments, and the jewish historian Josephus(37-95 AD) says that from these stones emanated a light as often as God was present. Writing about 400 AD, Saint Epiphinus, Bishop of Constantia tells of a marvellous *Adamas,* possibly a diamond, which by its appearance announced to the people the fate that God had in store for them.

In *Revelations Chapter 18,* referring to the building of the Holy City, the New Jerusalem, Saint John writes that the building of the wall was of jasper and the foundations of the wall of the city were garnished with all manner of precious stones. The first was jasper, the second sapphire, the third chalcedony, the fourth emerald, the fifth sardonyx, the sixth sardius, the seventh chrysolite, the eighth beryl, the ninth topaz, the tenth chrysoprasus, the eleventh jacinth and the tenth amethyst.

It helps to know that the importance of gemstones has been known since the earliest times, and that we can discover the lost knowledge and learn to understand the deep beauty and magic of the stones. We can allow them to develop our intuition and bring out the healing power latent in all of us. Here is a list of some of the stones with their meanings to help develop understanding, and again at the end of the book I have suggested further reading if you wish to develop in this area.

Agate	A fire sign, which helps to discover inner truth and is a powerful healing stone, particularly for the colon and the pancreas.
Amber	This stone helps to combat absent mindedness. It is fossilised in ancient trees and is noted to be good for the spleen and heart.
Amethyst	This is a beautiful love stone. It is very inspirational and is a powerful spiritual stone. It helps to raise the inner consciousness.
Aquamarine	This stone is a great mental and emotional balancer; it inspires love and peace. It strengthens the kidneys and cleanses the body.
Aventurine	A stone to strengthen the blood. It purifies the mental, emotional and etheric bodies. It inspires independence and good health.
Carnelian	The friendly stone. A healing stone that energises the physical, emotional and mental self. It creates a link with the inner self and brings joy, love and warmth.
Citrine	A quartz crystal which is known to be good for the kidneys and digestive organs. It helps to raise self esteem and gives hope and warmth.
Blue Lace Agate	A very delicate stone and one for healing. It strengthens the heart and improves self esteem. As it is a semi-precious stone it is a human stone and not a spiritual one. It is reputed to be able to help discover the sex of an unborn child.
Garnet	This stone has been nicknamed the 'day dreamer' because of its ability to enhance the imagination. It too is good for purifying the blood, and it is a stone that brings love.
Jade	Another healing stone that gives a sense of balance to the spirit. It aids the kidneys and the immune system. The stone is a giver of wisdom and courage.
Jasper	This too is a healing stone which in particular aids the bladder. It helps to balance the whole body and emotionally helps to keep the 'feet on the ground'.
Quartz (clear)	This is a very powerful stone. It is one which dispels all negativity in the energy field, and it receives and transmits energy. It is excellent for healing and for attuning with the higher self.
Rose Quartz	The stone of love. It is a stone that helps to let go of anger and brings forgiveness and compassion. It helps to build self-respect, and is said to increase fertility.

Each sign of the zodiac has stones related to it. These birthstones are part of an intricate inner relationship, and are an integral part of a horoscope. Personal stones may be found in the list following.

Aries (Ram)	Jasper, Ruby.
Taurus (Bull)	Lapis Lazuli, Rose Quartz, Sapphire.
Gemini (Twins)	Carcinia, Rock Crystal, Tigers Eye.
Cancer (Crab)	Chalcedony, Emerald, Serpentine.
Leo (Lion)	Chrysolite, Diamond, Quartz Crystal.
Virgo (Virgin)	Agate, Carnelian.
Libra (Scales)	Aventurine, Emerald, Jade.
Scorpio (Scorpion)	Beryl, Bloodstone, Garnet.
Sagittarius (Archer)	Citrine, Topaz.
Capricorn (Sea Goat)	Jet, Smokey Quartz.
Aquarius (Water Bearer)	Lapis Lazuli, Malachite, Turquoise.
Pisces (Fishes)	Amethyst, Moonstone.

My feeling is that in the end you will select the stones that you get an inner feeling for, and that you are instinctively attracted to. Once you have chosen your stones, they must be looked after; they must be cleansed after working with them, and they respond to being outside in the full moon, as it re-energises them. The stones are living vibrations which can surround and affect our everyday life; don't be afraid to talk to them, wear them, use them for meditation, and if you have stones that feel very personal to you, keep them for yourself, don't let them be touched by others as this could interfere with the special relationship you have built up. Stones pick up the vibrations, both positive and negative of those who handle them, which is why they need cleansing after use, and why if you have your own special unity with a particular stone, then it is for you and you alone.

To cleanse stones put them under running water and ask that all negativity flow from them, then turning them with the point upwards, if there is one, ask that they be filled with love and healing. Alternatively, take deep breaths and imagine that a white light is coming in through the top of your head and out with each breath; you can then breathe love and healing into each facet of the stone.

There are of course many more stones and crystals than I have mentioned here, and there is much more to say about all of them, not least how they can work for and with each person. There are books devoted entirely to the stones which give an amazing insight into their power, and one or two are recommended in the booklist. Do search out books on all these subjects, as by reading you will increase your knowledge and share in the wisdom of those who have trodden the path before.

11 Conclusion

The aim of this book has been to introduce the reader to different ways of thinking about the purpose of life and to offer an insight into existence beyond the earth plane. There is no question that life does continue after death and the way we live life today will influence future incarnations. Karmic debt is a reality and should help us to understand the true purpose of life.

I have attempted to introduce basic pathways to spiritual development, but it goes without saying there are many others. In future books I will be introducing material which will further develop the thinking and spiritual progression.

In my journey I have found that the most significant aspect of my development came from reading widely the literature available, much of which I was led to by my guides and helpers. The importance of reading cannot be stressed sufficiently if spiritual development is the aim. As has already been stated, I include a short book list of recommended reading, but the reader should allow intuition to guide him to literature for his personal needs.

Meditation is also very important and a necessary discipline but I will write about this in another publication.

Finally I hope this book has provided a basis for individual development. Each must choose his own way, and I hope I have stimulated the urge to travel along new pathways which can only lead to greater personal fulfilment.

SEEK AND YOU SHALL FIND.

RECOMMENDED READING

Bailey, Alice, *Death the Great Adventure,* Lucis, 1985.

Bailey, Alice, *Esoteric Astrology, Lucis,* 1951.

Birkbeck, Lyn, *Sun, Moon and Planet Signs,* Bloomsbury, 1990.

Blavatsky, Helena, *The Secret Doctrine,* Theosophical Publishing House, First Published 1888.

Fortune, Dion, *The Mystical Qatalah,* Aquarian Press, 1970.

Frazer, Sir James, *The Golden Bough,* Macmillan, 1963.

Gibran, Kallill, *The Prophet,* Heinemann, 1956.

Goodman, Linda, *Star Signs,* St. Martin's Press, New York, 1987.

Holbeche, Soozi, *The Power of Gems and Crystals,* Judy Piatkus, 1991.

Kunz, George F., *The Curious Lore of Precious Stones,* Bell, New York, 1989.

Lemesurier, Peter, *Gospel of the Stars,* Compton Press, 1977.

Lind, Ingrid, *The Spiritual Teaching of White Eagle,* Aquarian Press, 1984.

Richelieu, Peter, *A Soul's Journey,* Aquarian Press, 1989.

Sadhu, Mouni, *The Tarot,* Unwin, 1962.

USEFUL ADDRESSES

The Arcane School,
Lucis Trust,
Suite 54,
3 Whitehall Court,
London SW1A 2EF.

Creative Being Centre, *(enquire about courses)*
30 Albany Road,
Stratford on Avon,
Warwickshire.

The Findhorn Foundation, *(a successful New Age centre)*
Forres, IV36 0RD,
Scotland,

The Greater World Spiritual Centre,
3-5 Conway Street,
London W1P 5HA.

The College of Psychic Studies,
16 Queensway Place,
London SW7 2EB.

The Spiritualist Association of Great Britain,
33 Belgrave Square,
London SW1X 8QB.

The Theosophical Society *(enquire for courses)*,
50 Gloucester Place,
London W1H 3HJ.

The Wrekin Trust *(Founded in 1971. They run courses and workshops)*.
Runnings Park,
Croft Park,
West Malvern,
Worcsestershire, WR14 4BP.

GLOSSARY

Akashic records They are to be found on the astral plane and are a historical record of everything that has occurred on the earth. Some mediums are able to tap into the records.

Astral level The realm entered by the spiritual part of man after death, and the dwelling of higher spiritual bodies. It is normally invisible to ordinary sight, and yet can be entered in a sleep state or in a state of altered consciousness.

Aura An energy field surrounding the human body emanating colours which differ according to each individual. Many psychics are able to see the aura and its colour.

Bailey, Alice Born in 1880, she founded the Arcane school which continues to promote her teachings. Her books, which were written when she was in touch with the masters over a period of 30 years, are still widely admired.

Besant, Annie 1847-1933. A remarkable woman, she devoted her life to working for the good of humanity and the world through the Theosophical Society.

Blavatsky, Helena 1831-1891. She was without doubt the most remarkable occultist of her time. She was co-founder, with Henry Olcott, of the Theosophical Society in New York 1875. Her most remarkable books are Isis Unveiled (1877) and The Secret Doctrine (1888).

Chakras Loosely translated, the Sanskrit word means 'wheel'. There are seven main chakras or energy points in the human body which can be aroused through meditation and by use of crystals.

Clairaudience The ability to hear sounds and spirit voices.

Clairvoyance 'Clearseeing'; ability to receive information by seeing mentally that which exists out of normal sight.

Cosmos The universe as a whole.

Esoteric	From the Greek word meaning 'inner', 'concealed', 'secret'. The esoteric doctrine expresses a relationship between man and the spiritually populated universe.
Essenes	A sect who lived by the Dead Sea 2,000 years ago and were responsible for the Dead Sea Scrolls.
Etheric	The magnetic field which surrounds the human body; it extends for about an eighth of an inch around each part of the body, even each strand of hair.
Great White Brotherhood	A group which has attained high spiritual perfection, and which includes masters such as Jesus and the Lord Buddha.
Karma	The law of reincarnation; it could be seen as the law of consequences when the fruits of action in one lifetime determine the condition of life in the next.
Medium (see also trance medium)	A person who has the ability to communicate with the spirit world.
Ouija board	Ouija is derived from the french and german words for 'yes', and was originally devised as a board game. Now it is used as a means of spirit communication but should never be attempted without the presence of a trained medium.
Paranormal phenomena	Events which lie beyond normal scientific investigation.
Tarot	A set of cards used for the purpose of prediction.
Theosophical Society	A society founded in 1875, its motto being 'There is no religion higher than the truth'. The name derives from the greek word 'theos' meaning 'god' and 'sophia' translated as 'wisdom'. Many of its teachings are based around Buddhism and also on knowledge received from ancient times. The works of Helena Blavatsky have proved to be foundation stones for the modern day theosophical movement.
Trance medium	A medium who communicates in a state of trance with spirit.
Transition	The point of death, when the spirit moves to a higher plane.